Horse Books:

The Ultimate Horse Book for Kids

100+ Horse & Pony Facts, Photos, Quiz and Word Search Puzzle

Jenny Kellett

Contents

Introduction

It's hard not to love horses! But how much do you really know about your favorite hooved friend?

In this book you will learn over 100 amazing new things about horses and ponies — from the elegant Arab to the shaggy Shetland. And then you'll have a chance to test your new-found knowledge! You'll be a horse expert in no time.

Are you ready? Let's go!

A horse and foal.

Horse Facts

Horses can sleep lying down or standing up!

• • •

Horses can see nearly 360° thanks to the position of their eyes on the side of their heads.

• • •

Horses have the largest eyes in relation to their heads of all land animals.

Foals can walk and run just hours after being born.

• • •

There are lots of names for horses! A female horse is a mare; a male horse a stallion; a young male horse is called a colt, and; a young female horse is a filly.

• • •

Horses are herbivores, meaning they only eat plants.

• • •

Horses have been used by humans for over 5000 years.

A young stallion.

A young foal taking a rest.

A horse has around 205 bones in its body. That's one less than in the human body.

• • •

There are around 60 million horses in the world.

Horses often make a facial expression that looks like they're smiling or laughing, but actually, they move their mouths this way to help them smell better.

• • •

Although some people think that horses are colourblind, they are not. However, they can see yellows and greens better than purples and violets.

• • •

Horse hooves are made from the same protein that human hair and fingernails are made from — keratin.

The Zaniskari or Zanskari is a breed of small mountain horse or pony from Ladakh district India. *Image: Zaniskari Horse in Ladhak, Jammu and kashmir.jpg from Wikimedia Commons by Eatcha, CC-BY 4.0*

When a horse gallops all four of its hooves are off of the ground, meaning they're almost floating!

• • •

There are over 300 different breeds of horses.

• • •

The oldest breed of horse is the Arab.

• • •

Horses have great memories. Some scientists say that it's even better than an elephant's.

How tall is that horse? When measuring a horse you do it in hands, rather than feet or inches. One hand is 4 inches. Horses that are under 14.2 hands in height are usually (but not always) ponies.

• • •

Horses are famous for their large teeth! In fact, their teeth take up more space in their heads than their brains do.

• • •

Male and female horses have a different amount of teeth. Male horses have 40 teeth, while females have only 36.

The average lifespan of a domestic horse is around 25 years, however, in the 19th century a horse called 'Old Billy' is said to have lived to the ripe old age of 62!

In more recent times, 'Sugar Puff' lived to the age of 56 and died in 2007.

• • •

There is only one truly wild breed of horse in the world: the Przewalski's horse. The only wild population lives in Mongolia.

A Shetland pony.

Horses are very expressive. They use their ears, eyes, and nostrils, as well as facial expressions to express their mood.

• • •

Horses in groups never lie down at the same time. At least one will always stay on the lookout for any potential dangers.

• • •

An adult horse's brain weighs approximately half of a human's: around 0.9 kg (2 lb).

Wild horses in Kosovo. *Credit: Aljabakphoto*

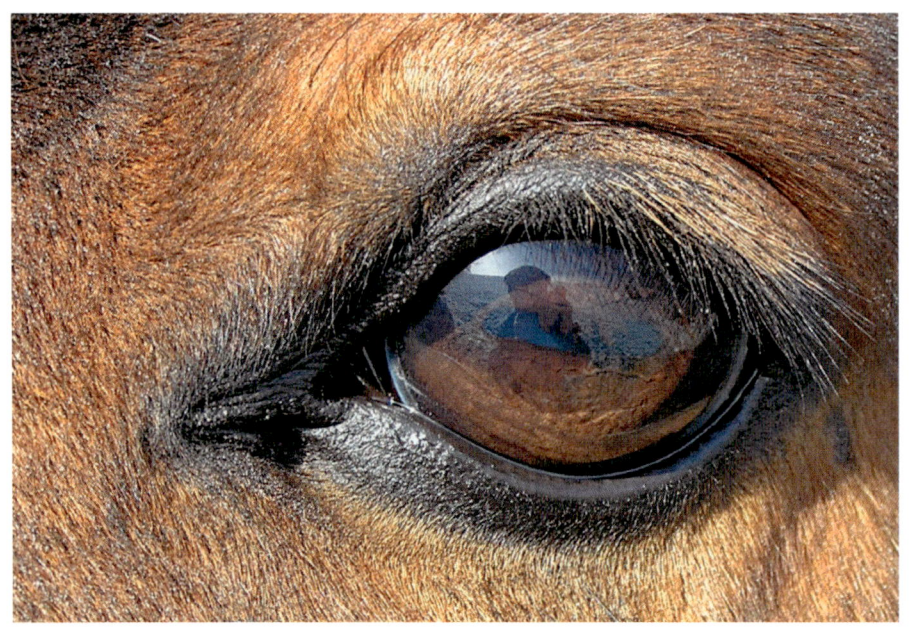

Close-up of an eye of an Andalucian horse.

It's impossible for horses to burp or vomit.

• • •

In 2003 a horse was successfully cloned in Italy.

• • •

Horses really like sweet flavours, and will probably reject anything that's too sour or bitter.

• • •

Every day, horses produce around 37 litres (10 gallons) of saliva.

An average horse heart weighs 4-4.5 kg (9-10 pounds).

• • •

Horses with pink skin can be prone to sunburn.

• • •

If a horse loses a hoof, it can take 9-12 months for it to fully grow back.

• • •

Hot tip! Don't use a red ribbon on a horse's tail, as it will make it kick.

American Quarter Horse, Bay. *Credit: Rumo*

Is your horse cold? Feel the back of their ears and if it's cold there, then the whole horse feels cold.

• • •

Horses have been cross-bred with zebras, to produce a zorse.

• • •

In a group of horses, the dominant female always takes the lead — not the male.

• • •

A horse's father is called a sire and the mother of a horse is called a dam.

A Zorse in a zoo in Germany. Credit: Fährtenleser

Horse breeds can be divided into three categories: hot bloods, cold bloods and warm bloods. These are decided based on different characteristics of the breed, including speed, endurance and how suitable they are for riding.

• • •

Hot bloods are the fastest type of horse and are used in racing. Cold bloods are strong and are used for hard work such as farming. Warm bloods are a combination of strong and fast, making them ideal for everyday riding and competitions.

A chestnut Gypsy Cob horse. An example of a cold-blooded breed.

Icelandic horses may be small and look like ponies, but they are actually horses.

Ponies aren't only just small horses. They often have thicker manes, tails and coats. Their body shapes are different, and they also usually have much calmer temperaments.

• • •

The gestation period for a horse (the length of time it is pregnant) is around 340 days.

• • •

Horses usually only have one foal. Twins are very rare.

Although horses can become pregnant at 18 months, it is most common for them to be allowed to breed after the age of three.

• • •

Horses are trained to be saddled and ridden between the ages of two and four.

• • •

Horses are a one-toed animal. However, this wasn't always the case. Ancient ancestors of the horse had multiple toes.

The first-ever female jockey was Diane Krump in 1969. Still, very few women become jockeys compared to men.

• • •

Hooves never stop growing. That's why domesticated horses need to have their hooves trimmed every five to eight weeks. Horses in the wild naturally wear down their hooves due to the terrain.

• • •

Horses have good hearing, partly thanks to their ears, which can rotate up to 180°, giving them near 360° hearing without having to move their head.

A female rider practicing in an arena.

Horses have a great sense of proprioception. That's a big word! It means they unconsciously know where their body and limbs are at any time.

This is important as they are classed as prey animals, meaning they need to be fully aware at all times to protect themselves from predators.

• • •

Horses can be fussy eaters! Their strong sense of taste means they can sort through hay and fodder and choose what they like the best.

Two horses eating from the ground.

Horses have five natural speeds: walk, trot, pace, canter and gallop. They range from 5-48 km/h (3.1 - 30 mph).

• • •

Horses are curious creatures and they love exploring areas and things that they haven't seen before.

• • •

In early modern American history, stealing a horse was considered a hanging offence.

• • •

Horses have strange sleeping patterns.

They don't enjoy a nice long night's sleep like us humans. Instead, they take many shorter rests throughout the day. The average daily sleep time of a domestic horse is only 2.9 hours.

• • •

Arabian horses have one less vertebra than other breeds.

• • •

Although horses can sleep standing up, they can only reach REM sleep while lying down. REM (Rapid Eye Movement) sleep is the deepest kind of sleep, and it's when you have the most dreams.

The Tokara Pony is native to the Takara Islands of Japan. *Credit: TANAKA Juuyoh*

Horses have been used in wars since between 4000-3000 BC.

• • •

Horses can be used as a form of therapy. Therapeutic riding can be used by disabled people to help improve their balance, coordination, self-confidence and sense of freedom.

• • •

Being a jockey is a tough job! Jockeys may have to ride 12 different horses every day, many of which have very different temperaments.

Most white horses are actually grey. They are born a darker colour and turn white as they get older. If this is the case, they are called grey horses.

• • •

Shetland ponies may be tiny, but they sure are mighty. They are amongst the strongest breeds of small ponies.

• • •

Shetland ponies have been around since the end of the last Ice Age.

• • •

The horse's closest relative is a rhinoceros.

She's may not be not as white as she looks!

When a horse is resting its breathing rate is only about four breaths per minute.

• • •

There are no native horses in North America anymore. All horses have descended from European breeds. However, there is fossil evidence that horses were once native there over 8,000 years ago.

• • •

The fastest speed recorded for a horse was 88 km/h (55 mph).

The scientific name for the horse is
Equus Ferus caballus.

• • •

There are many different colours of
horses. Some of the most common are:
Bay, Chestnut, Grey, Black, Sorrel, Dun,
Palomino and Pinto.

• • •

Horses are still used by policemen
around the world today. They are often
used to break up large crowds.

A palomino horse galloping.

American Quarter horses are a popular choice for cowboys and ranch workers.

Just as human life expectancy has increased, so has equine life expectancy. This is thanks to advances in medicine and veterinary science.

• • •

Horses can grow moustaches! Next time you see a Gypsy Vanner horse, check out its furry upper lip.

• • •

The world's most popular breed of horse is the American Quarter horse.

Horses have really grown over the millennia! The earliest horses are believed to have been no bigger than a Golden Retriever.

• • •

Have you read the book Black Beauty? The author, Anna Sewell, wrote the book "to induce kindness, sympathy, and an understanding treatment of horses".

• • •

In most competitions, horse jockeys are not allowed to be the owners of the horse they are riding.

An Icelandic horse showing us his teeth.

The most expensive horse ever bought cost $70 million. Fusaichi Pegasus was a Thoroughbred racing horse and he won the Kentucky Derby in 2000.

• • •

Scientists believe that horses can read human facial expressions.

• • •

The rarest horse is the Sorraia, which comes from Portugal. There are less than 200 left in the wild.

• • •

The smallest horse ever recorded was only 35.5 cm (14") tall! His name was Einstein.

Horses need to eat regularly as food leaves their stomachs quite quickly, and if left too long without food, stomach acids start eating away at the layers of tissue inside.

• • •

Horses are thirsty creatures! They drink 19-37 litres (5-10 gallons) of water per day.

• • •

Unlike many other animals, horses can not be albino.

• • •

There are horses on every continent of the world except Antarctica.

The highest ever jump recorded by a horse was in Chile in 1949. Huaso jumped 8 feet, 1 ¼ inch!

. . .

Although it may seem like horses will eat anything, there are some common fruits and vegetables that you definitely shouldn't feed them. These include persimmons, rhubarb, onions, potatoes, tomatoes, avocados and cabbage.

. . .

The town of Love Valley, North Carolina has a no-cars policy. Instead, residents travel everywhere on horseback.

A competitor in the 2015 HITS Winter Classic in Tucson, AZ. Credit: Gene Devine

A thoroughbred racehorse wearing its bridle in the snow. Credit: Sheri Hooley

There are many amazing movies based on horses. Some of the most popular ones include *Dreamer, Secretariat, National Velvet, The Horse Whisperer* and *Racing Stripes.* Which one is your favourite?

• • •

Just how smart are horses? Some scientists have estimated a horse's intelligence to be the same as that of a 3-year-old human.

• • •

Cowboys generally ride American Quarter horses.

Horses come from the *Equus* genus. In this family are also donkeys, *Equus asinus*; the mountain zebra, *Equus zebra*; plains zebra, *Equus quagga*; Grévy's zebra, *Equus grevyi*; the kiang, *Equus kiang*; and the onager, *Equus hemionus.*

• • •

Horses weren't quite so comfortable to ride before saddles came along! However, they've been around longer than you might think. They were invented in 365 AD by the Sarmatians. Since then, saddles have become much more advanced and can be made from many different types of materials including fibreglass and carbon fibre.

The bridle came long before the saddle. The earliest evidence of the use of a bridle was around 1400 BC, and they were made of rope, bone and wood. Around 200 years later, bronze started to be used.

• • •

What do those annoying horse flies have to do with horses? Not that much, actually! However, they do have a preference for annoying large animals like cows and horses.

• • •

Mares will feed their foals milk for several months.

When foals are born their legs are almost the same length as they will be when they are an adult!

• • •

If a horse is made up of several different colours, it is said to have broken colour.

• • •

Horses can't breathe through their mouths.

• • •

Horses burn more energy lying down than they do standing up.

A foal in Serbia. Credit: Valentin Salja

Horse Quiz

Now test your knowledge in our Horse Quiz! Answers can be found on page 67.

1. What is the most popular breed of horse in the world?

2. Name 3 fruits or vegetables that horses shouldn't eat.

3. It is common for horses to give birth to twins. True or false?

4. What animal can you breed with a horse to create a Zorse?

5. Why don't groups of horses all lie down at the same time?

A blue-eyed broken colour horse.

Credit: Sheri Hooley

6. There is only one truly wild breed of horse in the world. Can you name it?

7. At what speed must a horse be going to have all of its hooves off of the ground?

8. How many breeds of horses are there?

9. How many teeth does a horse have?

10. In which position do horses need to be sleeping in in order to have dreams?

11. Horses eat meat. True or false?

12. What is the name of the protein that horse hooves are made of?

13. How old was Sugar Puff when she died in 2007?

14. It's impossible for horses to burp or vomit. True or false?

15. How much saliva does a horse produce per day?

16. How long does it take a horse hoof to grow back?

17. What colour ribbon should you not use in a horse's tail if you don't want to be kicked?

18. Which type of horse is best for racing? Warm blood, hot blood or cool blood?

19. What is the gestation period for a horse?

20. How many toes does a horse have?

A warm blood horse. *Credit: Luisa Peter*

Answers:

1. The American Quarter horse.

2. Persimmons, rhubarb, onions, potatoes, tomatoes, avocados and cabbage

3. False.

4. Zebra.

5. There always needs to be at least one horse keeping a watch out for predators and danger.

6. The Przewalski's horse

7. A gallop, about 40 to 48 km/h (25 to 30 mph)).

8. Around 300.

9. Male horses have 40 teeth, while females usually have 36.

10. Lying down.

11. False. They are herbivores.

12. Keratin.

13. 56.

14. True.

15. 37 litres (10 gallons)

16. 9-12 months.

17. Red.

18. Hot blood.

19. 340 days.

20. Just one.

HORSES
WORDSEARCH

G	F	S	J	F	E	D	S	A	S	D	V
W	B	R	I	D	L	E	W	G	F	D	E
E	T	I	E	G	M	D	Q	T	E	H	R
F	O	D	D	E	R	Y	Q	U	W	O	H
J	G	I	Z	Z	M	U	M	W	U	R	F
L	F	N	X	C	G	E	F	G	Y	S	S
F	D	G	A	L	L	O	P	L	D	E	I
N	S	Q	G	R	S	B	Q	W	G	S	H
Y	W	G	F	O	A	L	V	W	W	H	T
F	K	S	G	F	A	B	N	G	S	O	A
J	F	D	S	H	T	E	L	G	I	E	B
S	P	O	N	I	E	S	B	S	F	E	V

Can you find all the words below in the wordsearch puzzle on the left?

BRIDLE   GALLOP   EQUUS

ARAB   RIDING   PONIES

FODDER   FOAL   HORSESHOE

Sources

What Fruit & Vegetables Can Horses Eat?
Published: 19 January 2020, 02:40 by Sommer
Smith. Retrieved 2020-08-29.

**"Horses Can Read Our Body Language Even
When They Don't Know Us"**. 2020. Sciencedaily.
https://www.sciencedaily.com/release

**"Horse Facts And Worksheets For Kids •
Kidskonnect"**. 2017. Kidskonnect. https://
kidskonnect.com/animals/horse/# Retrieved 2020-
09-01.

"AQHA Annual Report - 2014 Horse Statistics".
American Quarter Horse Association. Archived
from the original on September 23, 2015. Retrieved
August 24, 2015.

Grubb, P. (2005). **"Order Perissodactyla"**. In
Wilson, D.E.; Reeder, D.M (eds.). **Mammal Species
of the World: A Taxonomic and Geographic
Reference** (3rd ed.). Johns Hopkins University
Press. pp. 630–631. ISBN 978-0-8018-8221-0. OCLC
62265494.

"Horse Mounted Unit". United States Park Police. National Park Service. Archived from the original on February 18, 2008. Retrieved 2020-09-03.

"See the town where cars aren't allowed, only horses!" www.horsehooves.com. Retrieved 2020-08-28.

"Do You Know How Horses Sleep?". 2020. The Spruce Pets. https://www.thesprucepets.com/learn-how-all-horses-sleep-1887328.

"The Horse – Your Guide To Equine Health Care". 2020. The Horse. https://thehorse.com/. Retrieved 2020-09-03.

"Rules of the Australian Stud Book". Australian Jockey Club Ltd and Victoria Racing Club Ltd. July 2008. p. 9. Retrieved 2020-09-03.

Ensminger, M.E. (1991). **Horses and Tack** (Revised ed.). Boston, MA: Houghton Mifflin Company. pp. 11–12. ISBN 978-0-395-54413-6. OCLC 21561287.

Mau, C.; Poncet, P. A.; Bucher, B.; Stranzinger, G.; Rieder, S. (2004). **"Genetic mapping of dominant white (W), a homozygous lethal condition in the horse (Equus caballus)"**. Journal of Animal Breeding and Genetics. 121 (6): 374–383. doi:10.1111/j.1439-0388.2004.00481.x

Johnson, Tom. **"Rare Twin Foals Born at Vet Hospital: Twin Birth Occurrences Number One in Ten Thousand"**. Communications Services, Oklahoma State University. Oklahoma State University. Archived from the original on 2012-10-12. Retrieved 2020-09-03.

Evans, J. (1990). **The Horse (Second ed.).** New York: Freeman. p. 90. ISBN 978-0-7167-1811-6. OCLC 20132967.

Sellnow, Les (2004). **Happy Trails: Your Complete Guide to Fun and Safe Trail Riding.** Eclipse Press. p. 46. ISBN 978-1-58150-114-8. OCLC 56493380.

Briggs, Karen (2013-12-11). **"Equine Sense of Smell"**. The Horse. Retrieved 2020-09-02.

Thomas, Heather Smith. **"True Horse Sense"**. Thoroughbred Times. Thoroughbred Times Company. Retrieved 2020-09-03.

Prince, Eleanor F.; Gaydell M. Collier (1974). **Basic Horsemanship: English and Western.** New York: Doubleday. pp. 214–223. ISBN 978-0-385-06587-0. OCLC 873660.

Examples are the Australian Riding Pony and the Connemara, see Edwards, pp. 178–179, 208–209

Pascoe, Elaine. **"How Horses Sleep"**. Equisearch.com. Archived from the original on 2007-09-27. Retrieved 2020-09-03.

"Home". **The Foundation for the Preservation and Protection of the Przewalski Horse.** Archived from the original on 2017-10-10. Retrieved 2020-09-03.

Pallas (1775). **"Equus hemionus"**. Wilson & Reeder's mammal species of the world. Bucknell University. Retrieved September 1, 2010.

"Introduction to Coat Color Genetics". Veterinary Genetics Laboratory. University of California. Retrieved 2020-09-03.

Ensminger, pp. 46–50

We hope you learnt some awesome facts about horses!

Follow us on our Amazon Author page for the latest book releases.

Manufactured by Amazon.ca
Bolton, ON

19686907R00045